VOLUME III

THE MAN
THE MYTH
THE LEGEND

Articles on the body's intelligence, inspired quotes, and recipes for regeneration.

BY ARNOLD KAUFFMAN

Quantity sales: Special discounts are available on quantity purchases by corporations, associations, and others. For details, contact the publisher.

Orders by U.S. trade bookstores and wholesalers:
Please contact Arnold's Way at

Arnold's Way
319 West Main Street
Suite #4
Lansdale, PA 19446

Tel: (215) 361-0116

For more information visit www.arnoldsway.com

Or visit Arnold's Way on YouTube & Facebook

First Edition

Printed in the United States of America

In this book, you will find essays that I (a professional dishwasher) have written, giving my opinion on the following topics:

Breast Cancer III

Cataracts

Changing Diet

Chemicalization

Chicken Pox

Chocolate

Colon Cancer

Commitment to Health

Constipation

Crutches

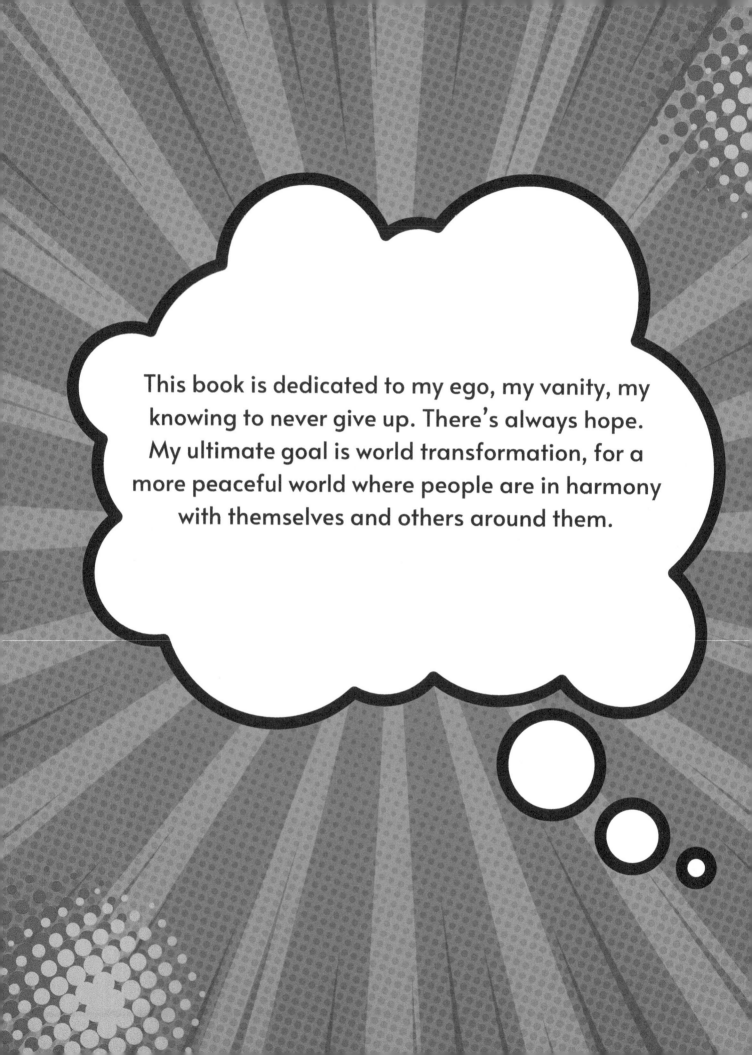

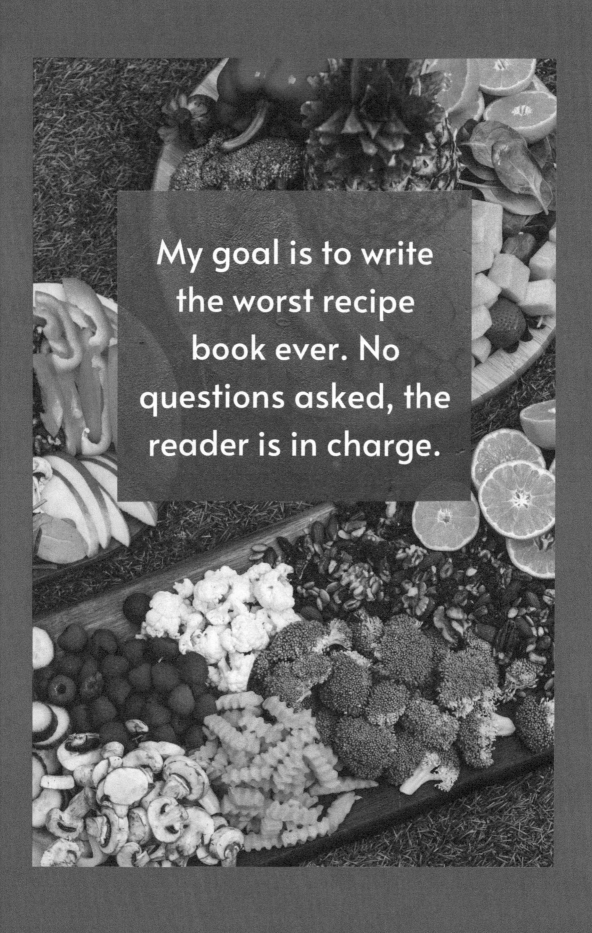

My goal is to write the worst recipe book ever. No questions asked, the reader is in charge.

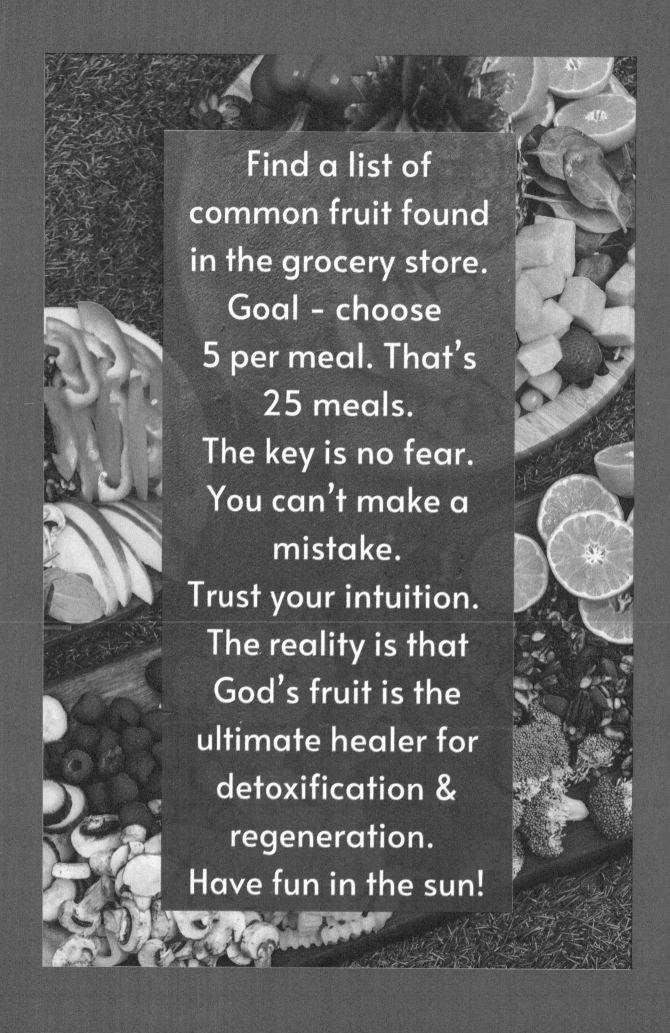

Find a list of
common fruit found
in the grocery store.
Goal - choose
5 per meal. That's
25 meals.
The key is no fear.
You can't make a
mistake.
Trust your intuition.
The reality is that
God's fruit is the
ultimate healer for
detoxification &
regeneration.
Have fun in the sun!

Breast Cancer - A Different View

written March 25, 2004

As the owner of Arnold's Way, a vegetarian raw cafe and health food store, I would like to share my views on breast cancer. From my perspective, breast cancer can not only be cured but is also totally preventable.

In those countries - as quoted by Dr. Joel Fuhrman in "Eat to Live" - that have a mostly grain, fruit and vegetable diet, cancer does not exist. In China, Colin Campbell did a detailed study on cancer and dietary choices, and found that cancer did not exist in provinces where meat was rarely consumed. Campbell found that the rate of cancer increased proportionately with meat consumption.

In the United States, our diet includes 40-60% of our calories as dietary fat, mostly animal in origin. Also a high percentage of our food is processed. The weight of this dietary fat plus the chemicals in our food, may equal 50 pounds per person per year.

Dr. Kristine Nolfi states very bluntly that "breast cancer disappears on a raw food diet."

Dr. Lorraine Day created the video "Cancer Doesn't Scare Me Anymore" and states that "doctors know that chemotherapy, radiation and surgery are not the answer to cancer."

Aware of these views, I believe that women need to be given true options - both medical and raw foods information. Women must become aware that cancer is simply a group of cells that are not under the jurisdiction of the brain.

As Dr. Herbert Shelton states, cancerous and non-cancerous tumors are "indurations characterized by a hardening and filling in of empty space. It is an increase in the fibrous element, otherwise known as scarring and encapsulation. This process engulfs toxic materials in a gelatinous hardened fibrous sac in order to isolate them from the rest of the body. This is commonly referred to as tumor formation. This is the last intelligent thing the body will do before the last and final stage of disease." In other words, tumors are created by the body as a defense strategy to deal with the onslaught of toxic material that we consume through food, drugs, air, water, or skin contact such as cosmetics.

In order to beat any disease, the body needs to be given the proper tools and relieved of the source of toxic material. The proper healing strategies include plenty of sleep, exercise, fresh air, a diet of mostly organic raw food, and the right attitude - the realization that our bodies have an innate healing system that was genetically designed to beat any virus or bacteria that has entered our system.

As we look at the world, filled with chemicals in our food, air, water, cosmetics, workplace, garden, drugstore, etc., we begin to realize why cancer is so rampant today. We begin to realize why the incidence of breast cancer in women has gone up almost four-fold in the last 50 years. We begin to realize why almost 15 million American women were diagnosed with fibroid tumors last year. When we learn that cancer does not exist in all cultures, we wonder why no one asks why? When we understand the power of our natural immune system to heal us, we wonder why current cancer treatments attack the immune system?

I believe that if enough vitality remains, our immune systems can overcome any disease with the proper sleep, exercise, fresh air, and a diet of mostly organic raw food.

I thank you for your time,
Arnold

"Once a commitment is made, it's a done deal no matter what."

HA HA
Choose 5 fruits.
Make 10 different
smoothies.

Cataracts
written October 4, 2002

It was a scandalous Summer retreat
The cotton candy – the caramelized apple
All in good fun – All taken as the thing to do
The clouds rolled by – slowly but surely
The games of old became the same as today
The fast food was just too slow
Who knows – who knew – it was such a blur
Being able just to see can be such a blast
Please someone take these cataracts away

It was one of those long Monday nights that the words began to flow. It was a week of thought, a week of enjoying every sight. These were the words that jumbled through my soul. These were the words that brought fear to my heart. These were the visions that brought ever so much clarity to my everyday living. I can see – no glasses – no blurs – no fear of any eye disease. I am humbled by my ability to see.

It was on that note that I chose this weeks' topic; my ability to see, to enjoy, to experience what true beauty is with every step, with every breath, with every wink of an eye. I could not imagine ever losing my sight, but others are not so lucky. As quoted in Prescription for Nutritional Healing, "cataracts are the number one cause of blindness". As a layman in the field of medical research who has researched over 50 major diseases, I always fall back to what is a safe possibility of treatment. Cataracts (what was I thinking of), I chose the Merck Manual 17th Edition as my best resource. As defined, "cataracts may be caused by aging, exposure to x-rays – heat from infrared exposure, systemic medication". A quick synopsis but this is what it is. As it appears quoting Prescription for Nutritional Healing, "when the lens of the eye becomes clouded or opaque it is unable to focus close or distant objects. This eye condition is called cataracts". These are not the words I want to read if I have cataracts for there are truths and these are true.

As a raw foodist, amateur medical researcher, I think about the whys. I think about how are cataracts beneficial. I think about what circumstances have to occur in order for our body to circulate its waste to our eyes. It happened just as thoughts became words. In Vision Victory by Diana Diemel, her words of probable causes become perfectly clear, "constipation is the mother of all disease". What doesn't leave, circulates! Images of brown, circle bombers zoom into unprotective areas. We close our eyes and hope for the best. We think not of the dead cow and its meaty part that have been consumed. We think not of the body's concerted effort for elimination by whatever means to wherever. The remedy is so simple. We think not of the dead chicken and its barbeque wings to go. We hold our breath as dead fish enters the conversation. As Good Samaritan we do not wish to see the harm we do by our dietary choices. The term cataracts as quoted by Dr. Herbert M. Shelton, "a clouding of the crystal lens beginning usually at one border and progressing slowly until complete blindness results".

Am I talking in parallels? Am I talking in straight? Is there a correlation between eating essentially dead animals and cataracts. Absolutely! The body's intelligence is based on a God Supreme that reeks of honesty and truth. If the truths of all truth is spoken, how readily do we want to see the cow being slaughtered, being driven to their deaths by these huge trailers; their scream just before unconsciousness by laser gun? We read of Paul Nison report in The Raw Life, as if we really want to know; as if we really want to see; as if the body is slowly clouding to remind not to destroy, to lead, not kill. The body intelligence uses the eyes as a storage area for excess waste caused by the eating of dead meat. In Mark Grossman O.D. LAC, Improving and Saving Your Sight Holistic Eye Care, there are healing possibilities. We begin to read but we shall not ignore what caused cataracts in the first place. Besides nutrition, there are vitamins and supplements believed to help reduce visual stress. This and other healing medication all treat the symptom not the cause. If we research the words, the language, the possibilities, the medical standard states unequivocally that "cataracts are treated by surgery" as quoted by the Merck Manual 17th Edition, "usual indication for cataract surgery includes maximally corrected vision and subjective visual impairment that prevents needed or desired activities". The words of success continued. The words of replace flow into the sentences of healing. There is no mention of healing possibility with food choices. There is no mention of fast, the words, as quoted by Dr. Herbert M. Shelton, "one simply fasts and the cataract is absorbed and removed. Easy enough! If surgery is used, it is common to wait until the cataract completely covers the eye.

We stop; we hold our breath, we think of all options. We think primarily of seeing life as is, not by word or description but by actual sight. As a layman in search of a cure I am open to all possibilities. I will change my ways in order to live happily, in order to improve my health, in order to be young not only in heart but also in age. We age when we have aged thoughts. We age when the language of getting old starts to infiltrate our bones manifested by our thoughts. We get the cataracts when the images of the universe are thrown in a helter skelter world of killing, broiling, frying, cooking, burning, and eating. All things, all vibration, all sights being understood clearly by our eyes; as quoted by Leonardo Da Vinci, "Who would believe that so small a space could contain the images of all the universe".

It is on this note we begin to explore the miraculous gift of sight. A gift not just of seeing but of life universal, creative genius. There are just no words to describe the joy of seeing. It is truly a gift of untold proportion that the average human being carries with them from the beginning of birth until the end. In World Medicine, the eyes, as quoted, "can perceive 10 billion gradients of light and seven million shades of color. No small number, no small accident—especially since it happens over and over again without time out! We take a further step towards understanding why sight occurs. As quoted, "the eye works by taking in light and transforming it into electrical impulses that are sent to the brain where 90 percent of vision occurs". As we speak of sight, we speak of ourselves, we are connected, and there are no accidents in sight as there are no accidents of blindness caused by cataracts. We have to live in peace with ourselves, that's the secret. I empower myself to be myself of purity in mind and in spirit.

I review the words of Marc Grossman in "Improving and Saving Your Sight" I review his words of wisdom. "You teach best what you need most to learn. What you seek, you are. What you desire, you have. You have all the time you need". There is quote after quote talking about the eternal laws written by universal spirit of what is and what will be.

The human eye is a highly complex organ. Those who know the mechanics of the eye and how it works estimate it has close to one billion working parts, its ability is not questioned, its glory is unsurpassed.

So, we watch the ball being pitched, we watch the young girl quietly get into her car, we watch the boy beating on his drum, we wait for the red light. We watch all these actions in silent ignorance not knowing that those light waves travel at 186,000 miles per second to reach our eye before we see the vision. As quoted in World Medicine by Tom Monte, "the eyes instantly focus on the waves of light by precisely adjusting various parts of the eye". All one billion parts all have their job to do in order for vision to occur. They are all doing their job with total precision, total accurateness happening all the time. The image is then sent to the brain". As quoted again in World Medicine, "the brain receives multiple images because the left and right eyes
perceive light from slightly different vantage points". To add a further dimension towards this totally complex anatomical miracle, the image is upside down because the light is refracted or bent within the eye". Our brain, my brain, your brain; put these multiple images that are totally many and upside down and make it right, clear, concise, without hesitation, at the rate of 186 thousand miles per second.

So, we review cataracts one more time, we think of surgery, which involves the surgical removal of the lens and the insertion of a plastic artificial lens. According to Merck Manual 17th Edition, there's a 95% success rate without complication, which is excellent considering how long one has to endure the cataracts. Also considering there is no hope according to American Medical Standards. The other option is to educate oneself; cost is no money—no expense.

We listen to the words of Dr. Harris Brody MD, AM, DO, CW, A natural hygienic doctor as he repeats, why cataracts? As quoted, "its coagulation of the protein. The liver is overloaded with all that protein consumption". Dr. Harris Brody further states the other major problem is protein digestion. The body being constantly barraged on a daily basis of excess protein, it depletes our natural acid that normally would break up the excess protein. As the liver becomes overloaded it has to pass this excess waste into other areas of the body, meaning the organs, the tissues, and ultimately the eyes causing the lens to lose its transparency and it eventually becomes increasingly opaque; hence cataracts.

As we begin, so we end. We write about differences. We write about the same. Each disease becomes like the mellowness of soft water snowflakes. There are answers of possibilities, there are answers of no-hope. As we research, as we become to know that the healing begins from within, that everything we need to know we already know. Thomas A. Edison was so right as quoted, "The doctor of the future will give no medicine but will interest his patients in the care of the human frame, in diet and in the cause and prevention of disease".

I thank you for your time,
Arnold

"It's not over till
the fat lady
sings."

5 Fruit:

Choose any.
Goal – 10 meals.
You can't make
a mistake.

Changing Dietary Lifestyle
written October 15, 2003

It was the hour before midnight. It was the snooze before the big awakening. It was a time when everything seemed right and nothing was wrong. It was on these thoughts that I begin-begin to vent; begin to espouse; begin to ponder. Why life? Why me?

It's a Saturday night where music becomes the sunny side of tomorrow's haze, like a leftover pie that begs for another day. I choose these words carefully for I have other thoughts. I think of my phone conversation with Matt Goodman who just finished walking fifteen hundred miles of the application trail. Not only for the quest, not only for the glory, but for the information that he has earned the right to share.

Matt beat M.S. in five months on a hundred percent raw food diet. He had been suffering for eight years. So I think of our conversation, about the hope, the glory of what actually works for reversing M.S. What Matt said could work not only for M.S., but could work for reversing any disease. Matt understands. His body understands, and his goal is to do whatever it takes to spread the message that eating a hundred percent raw food diet could not only reverse your disease but make you a finely tuned lean mean fighting machine.

I struggle with the time, now approaching the other side of midnight. I think of my daily encounters. I think of what I said or what I didn't say. I think of my visitation from a young woman who came to listen, to hear, to try to understand. Her story is not unlike any other story, except for one minor detail. She was diagnosed with a grapefruit tumor in her cervix area and was told she had to get it surgically removed in five days.

This young woman is only 35 years old, married, with two children. When she heard this, her whole world fell apart. Words were like stone blocks that chiseled marble shards into her body that would forever be imbedded.

The medical community tossed words around like glue to fly paper. Words like cancer, like no hope, like immediate surgical removal. These words she heard, were imbedded in her. These were the words that hung over her as she heard of a possible alternative that could reverse the tumor without surgery, without an invasive knife being thrust into her body. She sat down in my office, my little chair, in the mist of the café. I heard her story. I felt the pain.

I could only share what I know. I could only share what books I have read. I could only share the stories I personally know, such as that of my wife. A brave woman who was given a similar diagnosis, similar circumstances but not the immediacy of an operation. Lucky for her, she knew me. Lucky for her she knew of another option.

Although she knew, she did not want to realize. She felt at the time that the medical community could do no wrong. At that time she believed in their diagnosis, she believed in their test, she believed in their medication. She could not fathom that just by changing one's dietary lifestyle the tumors could be reversed. Not only the tumors could be reversed but also her lifestyle could take her to greater heights, greater well-being and a greater vitality for the zest of life.

I spoke my words to her. I spoke my knowledge and I shared the story of my wife. This happened five years passed, my wife through a strange circumstance, which was lucky for her, chose to go the medical round against my wishes. She believed in the system and had faith in her doctors. She was ready to do whatever it takes, whatever they said, to make her body right.

It is on that note that things changed. For her doctor, after giving all the tests, after giving the diagnoses of fibroid tumors on her neck, breast, and cervix area plus a mild mini stroke, was on vacation. My wife was asked a to come back a month later.

My wife decided to go on a three-week water/juice fast. The reason being that when the body no longer has to expend any energy for digestion it will go to that part of the body which is non-productive. Such as a tumor, which is group of cells that are engulfed in a semi-membranous enclosure.

The tumor was created for the highest good for my wife. Any time my wife ate food that was essentially dead, whether it be a chemical, or lifeless cooked food, the body could not use it. It had to store it in a manner least likely that affects her immediate well-being.

For three weeks time my wife went on this stringent lifestyle. Which by the way was medically supervised. The body's own infinite wisdom used the energy that it normally uses for digestion and began attacking the tumor and dissolving it. It's that simple, that pure, that easy. No money, no operation, no knife, no scary words like cancer, like breast cancer survivor.

This was my story that I shared with this young woman. I did my job. I had nothing to gain, no money to collect, no pills to sell. Just a simple job of trying to have the woman understand that her body is her temple and it has to be honored, by choosing the right lifestyle.

I thank you for your time,
Arnold

"What's important? What's not? We climb the hills of make-believe and decide always which way is best to go."

How crazy or sane is this:

5 Fruits
20 Meals

You are the genius.

Chemicalization
written April 3, 2006

It is a Friday morning when everything seems so perfect, so amazingly fantastic, so amazingly pure and so amazingly out of place. It is just too perfect. I am living in a world that I created. I am living in a world based on my thoughts, based on my feelings and based on the possibilities that wherever I am, it is a blessing to be there. I could do no wrong. I am living a dream of perfection in an imperfect society. I got up early not because I had to but because I wanted to. I rested enough. I had slept 5 and half hours and was well rested. I am living on a mostly raw, mostly blended diet of green smoothies. These are the foundations that enable me to see the sun shining thru my bedroom everyday. These are the foundations that enable me to hear the green plants speak to me in voices so clear and so radiantly, lovingly that it touches the bottom of my soul. Everything I do, everything I write and everything I breathe is in tune to the world around me. It is on this note that I begin this newsletter. I write of what should be rather than what is.

I write of my anger. I write of my frustration. I write of words that deal with the atrocities of chemicalization of the human body. I write of what I see. I write of what I hear. I write of customers who choose a chemical healing path rather than a raw food healing treatment. I write of words to understand without trying to underscore the value in free decision. I stand in silence as I swallow hard on these well-meant choices of medical treatments. I stand in silence and allow the loud vibration of my horrific anger to spread throughout the land. If thoughts can boomerang from one soul to another, let the drums roll and let the truth ring out so crystal clear to those who want to hear. I speak of my customers who are afraid of the language of trusting their innermost wisdom of doing the right thing. I speak of the word cancer being so casually passed around from one person than moving on to the next. This is the word that is being forced upon our society. This is the word that we have created to offset the goodness in life. This word offsets the darkness of light and changes it into the gloom of doom. This is one of those evil words that everyone wants to know whether they have it but doesn't want to know if they do. Cancer is one of those words, which blindsides hope into despair, the goodness of life into a dark evil tunnel without any light and a word to hear especially when it is placed on our shoulders. These are the words I am dealing with on a Friday morning when everything in my world seems so perfectly right.

I speak of Tom. I speak of Bill. I speak of Sarah. I speak of Mary. Day in and day out all these names roll into my presence and into my store. All these people, all these families and all these real vulnerable people are being given this name to be placed on the buxom of their souls. It's like a sharp butter knife plunged into their heart, into their brain and into their every word spoken. Every blood cell is drenched with that weight of it, never leaving. These are my thoughts and I can't get them out of my head on this Friday morning. I know the pain of knowing that word so intimately. I know that death sentence as it hangs on our every movement. I know that people just march into a medical facility seeking a magic bullet that will wash everything clean once again. That is the path chosen by most. That is the path that is easy to travel. That is the path that is so wrong because it takes the responsibility from self to them.

We stand in silence and watch them die, one by one. We stand in silence as we watch the Toms, the Mary's and the Bills as they sit down and expose their bodies to these horrific chemical-blasting machines. We stand in silence as these machines ooze their poisons into our bodies. We stand in silence as these medications of beknownst (no such word) power are allowed into our bodies as if they know where to go. We stand in silence as the will of the people are being strung out to die while they listen to the magic words that cancer is part of you now please accept.

I speak not of death, not of pain and not of sadness. I speak of sharing. I speak words that will encourage just someone, anyone of the insanity of trusting a machine or a drug as your only hope for salvation. I speak of the purity of life to someone, anyone, to realize that a machine that pours out toxic chemicals from its plastic walls into our bodies cannot save us. I speak my truth of medications that will destroy a healthy man so much in fact that no doctor or medical establishment would ever prescribe it to a vibrant happy individual because it would make him or her deathly sick. Though, they would not hesitate, not even for an instantaneous second, to prescribe a sick wounded individual who is given that life sentence of cancer, that same medication, to make them healthier. My friends, where is that logic coming from? I watch in horror as customer after customer believes in this logic. It's beyond all sense of normalcy. Chemotherapy destroys the body. There is no such thing as a little amount. I sit. I write. I am in total disbelief that day after day I see people walking with blind shutters to a slow death because they didn't believe strong enough in their own healing ability. I watch in silence as I see all the cancer that is growing like a time bomb in everyone's system. I sit and admire the plants, as they grow green in spirit and green in my heart.

We talk about cancer. We talk about exactly what it is. Our bodies understand that truth. Our bodies understand that lie. As soon as a food is cooked above a temperature of 125 degrees (don't quote me), all the life force of the food is cooked out. To be considered a food it has to meet six qualifications according to Dr Joel Robbins. It has to be in an organic state otherwise the body cannot assimilate it properly in the system. It has to have vitamins and minerals. This is needed for the energy of our being. It has to have water content. Our bodies are made up supposedly of 70 percent water. It has to have protein. We need this for muscle building. It has to have glucose. This is needed for the fuel of the brain. It needs a constant supply. The food also has to have essential fatty acids. My friends these are the six essential that the food has to have in order for our body to use it. These are the six requirements that are needed as a source of energy for our bodies to have the proper equipment to fight any incoming disease that enters our system.   This is what some scientific people call an alkaline state. The body needs to be alkaline in order for cancer to be destroyed. This theory has yet to be disproved. I know I am entering area where my expertise is not as good as it should be. I know I am saying words and sentences which could be a little beyond my reach. I have no choice in this matter. There are people dying out there because they are given the wrong information. There are people dying out there because they are given the wrong treatment. How in hell is a medication going to save anyone? How in hell does a medication know where to go? We have 98000 miles of arteries. Who directs that medication? How does the blood know what to do? Does a chemical reaction justify the side effects caused by this continuous flow of interaction?

I sit in silence. I think of truth as being everything alive, everything that is good and everything that we can eat. According to Dr. Joel Robbins, a food has to meet three qualifications in order for us to eat it (1) It has to grow in nature (2) It has to grow on a tree bush or vine or in the earth (3) you have to be able to eat it in large quantities in

a raw state. These rules are so simple to follow. There is no medication that grows in nature. It's dead and it has no life force and the body does not recognize it. It makes the body acid forming which is harmful to the body. It does not interact peacefully and lovingly within our body. Our body sees it as a harmful invader and tries to destroy it. Every time we ingest food that does not meet these qualifications the body considers it acid forming. This harmful invader will eventually begin mutating the cells causing them to be cancerous. By my definition, cancer cells are those cells that do not communicate with the body. They are uncontrollable with no sense of peace and harmony. Our body understands their harm and will destroy them giving the proper equipment. There is no cure for cancer. Period. There is no hope unless we abide by the system of peace and harmony.

I sit in silence knowing what I say does not matter to most if not all people. I sit in silence, as I know that most people will not take responsibility for their own health. I sit in silence and watch day in and day out people gorging themselves with cancerous food that will eventually destroy them. My friends, food is not meant to entertain us but to fuel us. It is that simple and that pure. Our bodies do not understand an onslaught of so many dead foods coming into its system day in day out. They cannot be neutralized fast enough so as not to have an effect. Protein takes 6 hours for the body to digest. You add a starch product, the body then would take days, if you're lucky, in order to digest that. Every time you eat a cookie, every time you eat a piece of bread, every time you eat dead food with ingredients, you are causing your body harm.

It is for this reason I push the green smoothie. I know what it can do. I have seen the results. I see the glow in peoples' faces once they begin drinking them on a regular basis. I see the energetic transformation of people who had no hope and begin to have hope. The simple ideal of ingesting fruit and leafy greens in a predigested state adds to our bodies immune fighting system. The simple act of our bodies not using much of its digesting energy, adds to our bodies immune fighting strength. The simple act of eating fruits and vegetables, which are alkaline forming all, helps destroy all this acid waste that was being accumulated in our system. The simple act of putting this liquid magic into our system helps our thought process to become clear and decide what is the right thing to do.

The secret for vibrant health is so simple, oh so pure and so easy to do. According to Loren Lockman, "What we can do is to provide the body with the optimum conditions in which to heal itself." This is what I believe. This is what I practice. This is what I tell all my customers. There is no magic pill. There is no magic machine. There is no one condition that will somehow change the body from a sick state to a healthy one. We need, as quoted once again from Loren Lockman's little pamphlet, A Handbook for Vibrant Living, "eight keys to optimal health fasting-sleep-diet-air-water-exercise-sunshine and emotional poise." These are the factors for good health. There are no others. These are the factors for treating all diseases. These are the choices that one has to make in order to recover from any disease, including cancer. These are the words that I share with all the Marys, the Toms and the Bills who want to go medically because they believe that their own body does not know how to heal. Close your eyes. Think of peace. Think of love. Think of what you want to do.

May peace be with you,
Arnold

"Life is always about win-win. Not I win-you lose. If one loses and the other wins, it's a bad deal. The key to life is to have both parties winning."

Think hard or don't think. Just do it:

25 meals from 5 fruits

Chicken Pox
written April 3, 2002

Raging bulldogs highlighted by the shadow of discontent
Amber fumes, purple hodgepodge that has no room
It was the voice of warning that no one took heed
Is 33 shot before two?
One too many or not quite enough?
Heed the voice of the well to do
Never ever is a nonsensible whimsical chord
The chicken pox vaccination has to be given this year to you

As March 2002 is about to end and April is about to begin, choosing a topic for the newsletter report becomes easier with hardly any thought. Having researched for almost one year straight, reading countless books, journals, medical texts plus many interviews, I didn't think there was anything that could surprise me. The many diseases that exist, the treatments for the ill, and the lifestyles we choose are all individually self-taught, for lack of a better work. Every question, every answer, becomes unified in united symbiotic unison. That is until I began my research of the chicken pox vaccination. Within the first hours of my reading, I was literally and figuratively thrown a right-handed fast curve that I barely avoided.

Randall Neustaedler, OMD stated in his book The Vaccine Guide: Making an informed choice, "The most frequently stated purpose of the chicken pox vaccine is not to protect children from this benign childhood illness but to keep parents at their jobs rather than missing a few days of work to care for their sick child at home." It was that statement that created a sensation of utter disbelief. It was that statement that drove me to research this week's topic.

This week we're on the quest for obtaining information regarding chicken pox, the vaccination, and my purpose for writing this. It started from a newspaper article I read titled "Chicken pox close to being wiped out."

Thinking to myself, if half presumptuous and half warily, let's not get hooked into believing everything I read.

I start to think, why am I doing this? This is really a no-brainer. As clearly stated in Vaccinations: Deception and tragedy by Michael Dye, "There is no evidence that your child will fare any better with the vaccination than without." From all reports that I read, "Chicken pox is universally recognized as a mild and benign disease of childhood," (from Vaccine Guide by Randall Neustaedler). Is wiping out this disease a good thing? These are questions that have to be answered. I stand, I sit. I look beyond the circle of clouds. We as parents are forever protecting our kids but at what cost? Dr. Mendelsohn, author of How to Raise a Healthy Child in Spite of Your Doctor, states, "There is growing suspicion that immunization against relatively harmless childhood diseases may be responsible for the dramatic increase in autoimmune diseases since most inoculations were introduced." To add further insult to the already supposedly innocuous chicken pox vaccine that the public so readily accepts, Dr. Mendelsohn further states, "The greatest threat of childhood diseases lies in the dangerous and ineffectual efforts made to prevent them through mass immunization. There is no convincing scientific evidence that mass inoculations can be credited with eliminating any childhood disease."

These are the statements that lead me into answering that question about why I am doing this. There is a red flag that has to be raised saying, "Stop the lies!" Our children's lives are affected. In today's world by the time a child is 18 months old they have received 25 vaccinations. There's a stance that we as parents have to make. Are we being told the truth about vaccinations? According to the British Association for the Advancement of Science childhood diseases declined by 90% before mandatory vaccine programs. In the book Vaccines: Are they really safe? by Neil Miller, we read that there were decreases in, "tetanus by 99.8%, diphtheria by more than 90% between 1900 and 1930, the pertussis death rate by more than 75% from 1900 to 1935, and the measles death rate 97.7% from 1900 to 1955." These are declines not advances. These are facts that we as parents have to consider when deciding whether or not our child should be vaccinated.

As I research the origin of the chicken pox vaccine it's like treading through murky water. There is a massive amount of deceptions and lies where the only truth that really stands out is the inconceivable of the vaccine actually becoming a reality.

Everybody, every book, agrees that chicken pox (varicella) is harmless. The symptoms of chicken pox as stated in the Vaccine Guide include "fever and runny nose followed by the appearance of small, flat, pink areas which soon fill with a clear fluid then open and crust over within 2-3 days." These symptoms are the impetus for the chicken pox vaccine. These same symptoms were why for so many years the authorities were reluctant to approve the vaccine. There was no justification for mass inoculation. The symptoms did not justify the adverse reaction the vaccine may cause. But all that is beside the point. It really doesn't matter. It's a financial decision, and our children's health is being played as a pawn. Once again I repeat my initial shock about the reason for the chicken pox vaccine, this time quoted by Neil Miller in Immunization Theory vs. Reality. "Nevertheless, medical forces are prepared to approve it because the US could save five times as much as it would spend on the vaccine by avoiding the costs incurred by moms and dads who stay home to care for their sick children." I read these quotes, and I'm at a total loss for words. I want to gobble up everything that sits before me. I throw up my hands, slam my fist, wishing to know why. There are no words to explain how these injustices not only became the law of the land but our constitutional justification of righteousness. There are no arguments, only a common consensus, which is yes, chicken pox vaccine is necessary and we the people are winning the war. Who owns these newspapers? Are their reporters reading the same journals and books that I'm reading? Are we living in two different centuries? In the Vaccine Guide, Randall Neustaedler tried to give an objective report on every vaccine, even to the point of bending over backwards on most vaccinations so he wouldn't rock anyone's boat. That is until he analyzed the chicken pox vaccine. The chicken pox vaccine "qualifies as one of the great marketing scams of the century. The idea of preventing chicken pox in healthy children is ludicrous to the point of insanity."

The quotes in this newsletter are from those that know, that study, and that live with the results, the deaths, the illness, and the prolonged adverse reactions of after the fact. They have no vested interest other than telling the truth from their perspective. Merck, the pharmaceutical giant that invested over 5 million dollars in its development, would like a return on its investment. These are the battles that are being fought, and these are battles throughout the country. They are in the hospitals, in the schools, in the daycare centers, and in the doctor's offices. Who will be responsible for the payback for all the millions of dollars being invested for drug research? Who will be the distributors for their merchandise? Who will lead the way? Who will believe us? These are the questions that have to be asked by those that are in the know before a single penny is spent.

In terms of vaccines, in the American medical establishment that is also a no-brainer. As stated by Randall Neustaedler, OMD, "The selling of this vaccine to the American public could only be due to an unequivocal belief that any vaccine is worthwhile." These are the assumptions of the pharmaceutical giants. Their financial commitment is too great for them to see it any other way. So we hold these thoughts in limbo. We also hold the fact that on March 17, 1995, the Food and Drug Administration announced that it approved a chicken pox vaccine. We also slightly disregard that shortly thereafter the American Academy of Pediatrics began recommending it for all infants. We also slightly submerge the following into our subliminal consciousness: the risk of death from chicken pox complications in healthy children is 0.0014. That in its own right is insignificant. If all these facts began to add up the reality of what is maybe really isn't. The fact that vaccines have been credited with saving millions of lives as stated by the powers that be is ludicrous to me. I, Arnold, only 1 week into my research have seen otherwise. But that's me. The research is not medical jumble gumble. It's easy to find, easy to figure out, easy to understand.

"Truth in all its kinds is most difficult to win, and truth in medicine is the most difficult of all."
-Peter Mere Latham
(from Shot in the Dark Harris L. Coulture and Barbara Loe Fischer)

I am totally exasperated. Every book I read speaks of the danger in vaccination. Am I a blind man following the faith of a heated dog? Are there shotguns of light that silhouette the darkened skies, or are we a nation of obedience? Are doing the right thing by not even questioning all this toxic material being put into our children's bodies for the sake of health?

I reread Vaccinations: Deception and Tragedy by Michael Dye. The word oxymoron filters through my every thought as I question in agreement his statement, "The assumption is often made that the only available protection against disease is from a series of pharmaceutically manufactured vaccines mandated by our government." Michael Dye states emphatically, "This is not the case." Absolutely, we me, you, have come from a higher power. Call it what you may, God, universal spirit, but whatever form it exists, it creates, it understand unequivocally. We came into this world with perfection with symbiotic unison of a total nation of cellular jubilation. Our immune system is a gift of immense intelligence and made to last during our lifetime from birth to death. In the infinite wisdom there is never a mistake. We have 100 trillion cells that not only make up our body, they have the ability to regenerate and create new life. As stated by Michael Dye, "This regeneration is the true source of healing, and it is how life is perpetuated. Your body creates about a million new cells every second."

So when a child develops a fever, let's rejoice in the body's effort to destroy an enemy invader. Perhaps raising the body temperature makes the inner environment hostile to the invading organism. When a child has a runny nose it is not necessarily bad. It is our body's immune system working frantically through every means possible to reject, to destroy, to encapsulate the enemy and send it on its way. Through mucous as the vehicle and the nose as the outlet this is our God-given forces of life, forces of regeneration, forces of perpetual perfection that created this ability of continual cleansing.

The lymph system is our protector, our army, and our self-defense. It makes up 2% of our total body weight and it is capable of protecting the other 98%. I read Michael Dye's description of the incredible immune system. I read Tom Monte's description. I read Al Carter's words in the Cancer Answer. I want to cry, laugh, scream, go to the hilltop, and sing their praises. It is that magnificent. All the glory that exists inside us for our good, for our protection. It's just so, so much! "Everyday millions of new red and white blood cells are born inside our bone marrow and these cells are sent where ever they are needed by our lymphatic and circulatory system. These are our armies of unequivocal loyalty. They are trained to undermine this holy bond with our higher power. In my opinion it is sacrilegious to quote that chicken pox is down 79%. It undermines the true intent of self-rejuvenation. These chicken pox occurrences are the forces of nature that have been our self-preservation since the beginning of time. I honor its presence within my soul. The chicken pox vaccine as been quoted, as been universally accepted, does not represent a threat. It should consider that as a gift. The body's innate intelligence is trying its utmost to cleanse itself. I thank you.

We gather as pawns against the wind and trees that gather their force from sky blue as infinite tales that hold its truth high for Mother Nature to spread her protective wings against our brow. I write, I share, and I allow what has to be seen, seen. It is my job. It is my passion. It is my love for who I am. It is the father in me.

I thank you for your time,
Arnold

References:
A Shot in the Dark by Harris Coulture and Barbara Loe Fischer
World Medicine by Tom Monte, East West Natural Health
Vaccine Guide by Randall Neustaedler, OMD
Immunization: Theory vs. Reality by Neil Z. Miller
Immunization: The People Speak by Neil Z. Miller
Vaccinations: Deceptions and Tragedy by Michael Dye
"Chicken Pox Close to Being Wiped Out," article by Susan Fitzgerald

"Vacation City is always in the now."

Great balls of fire:

Every piece of fruit can be a meal

Chocolate
written May 6, 2006

It is the first of May when I begin this months newsletter I could of written about a 100 different subjects In the art of healing oneself, the list is endless. In fact there is no end. What I thought and what I actually wrote apparently worlds apart were in reality the same statement I thought I was going to write about the over indulgence of chocolate not so much of its benefit but why not it should be eaten. It was one out of the blue by gosh holy Toledo thoughts that zoomed into my being about two days ago 15 minutes before I was supposed to arrive at work. I, Arnold, who up to until two-day s ago had barely even an opinion on chocolate, had now becoming a newborn chocoholic reformer. I wanted to share this eye-opener awakening wisdom with everyone. I, for whatever reason, had become smitten on the idiocy of thinking chocolate is good for one's soul, good for one's body and good for eating it with reckless abandonment. I, Arnold owner of Arnolds Way, wanted to create a happenstance; if not stopping people from eating chocolate at least warn them to moderate their intake.

I, who just two days ago, was literally driving down the street minding my own business enjoying the sun, the peace and the quietness of a town that hasn't really lost it's boyish charm .It was that type of a small town who's change could barely measure a small hiccup let alone an eye-opener awakening on the evils of chocolate. It was that type of day when all of a sudden for no reason other than the sky falling and great big lizard was splattering on windshield. These big bang ruinous thoughts entered into my domain of being. The words stated loud and clear that chocolate is bad. I said to myself like where did these words come from. These thoughts should not be entering into my head on this beautiful day in a quiet town just minutes from work. What I thought and what became reality became more bizarre after each passing minute.

I arrived at the store slightly late, slightly flabbergasted and slightly not sure that what I saw was really what I saw. It was customer waiting for me at my store. I stared at her and she stared back. It was one of those Fellini movie upstages where everything that was real became surreal. I had no idea what to expect. I then heard her words rumbling into me like molten steel coming out of it's hot drum. These were the roars of an epiphany that struck my core of recallective consciousness. She said "I want a chocolate shake. I have been thinking about it all morning." I was somewhat taken aback especially since these thought on the evils of chocolate were fresh in my memory. I stood defiantly against the wind raised myself taller than I have ever been (5'8" as compared to 5'7") and said "no, I will not serve you chocolate". I was somewhat taken aback by my reply and seriously taken aback by her reply. She stated" Arnold thank you I really didn't want to order that it was just on my mind." Ten minutes later another young woman walked in; To say she was white as a sheet would be an understatement, to say she was half out of it and half not there would be as close as a picture of what she looked like as a fair picturesque statement. In other words she was sick. She had one of those migraines that literally stopped her world from even existing. She was in pain and didn't know what to do. All these things I saw, I felt and the most amazing part was I knew what to say and what she should do to rid her body of those evil strangulations of her being. I knew her from being at my store literally everyday and ordering the same thing: a banana whip with lots of chocolate. I couldn't believe it my second hard luck side effect story on the over indulgence of chocolate in the first ten minutes .I stared her in the eye and said point blank, "I am not serving you chocolate today or any other day" .You would have thought she would be angry. You would have thought she would have made some type of protest. All these thoughts that should have happened didn't and all these things that didn't happen did. She said, "thank you, I will not only pass on the chocolate today I will not eat it any more." I thought I was in a surrealistic movie ensemble that all my thoughts on the evils of eating chocolate were surfacing like ants looking for a hide-away to crawl to. If two stories were not enough to convince me on at least warning my customers of not eating chocolate in excess, Lo and behold I received a phone call at 10:30 am. It was my third customer contact of the day. It was a customer who I have known for least 8 years. I knew he was eating a mostly raw diet and had made a miraculous recovery from a life threatening disease by changing his dietary habits.

What I thought I knew of his miraculous recovery was now not only being sabotaged but also completely being squashed. I listened to his words. I listened to his complaints. I listened to his frustration, his pains and his not knowing what to do as the long stories of all his major symptoms that once disappeared were now returning in greater numbers. What he was supposed to be doing and what he was doing was being precisely destroyed by the simple addition of 8 heaping teaspoons of chocolate to his morning green smoothie. I was flabbergasted listening to his story. I was flabbergasted listening to his illness that would eventually destroy him. I was flabbergasted mostly on what I was hearing. He was adding to his green smoothie. I was flabbergasted for lack of a better word. I stated one word and only one word to him" Stop": He had to stop the madness and the insanity of adding this supposedly super food into his daily green smoothie. I said point blank to him, "You are literally destroying your self with these 8 additional teaspoons of chocolate."

That was my chocolate stories on that Tuesday morning in my first half hour of work. I could have added my reflux story or breast cancer or a hundred other little antidotes of the different disease that come my way and stories of different people who are disobeying the laws of nature and paying a hefty price. Our lives are meant to be of vitality of beauty of being in the moment and enjoying the essence of our existence like a new born child that comes into the world full of hope and joy.

It is on that note that I give thanks to my daughter, Maya. The rest of the newsletter is dedicated to her. She has the one story which is my pride, my glory and which makes me the most proud. Maya has taught me the secrets of why health and why disease. It is based on one word and only one word that is part of her every movement, the love of thyself. This is the universal gift to her and to ourselves and we should be thankful for our every existence. There is no greater reward. Every word, every bite and every thought should be with a loving thought otherwise its toxic. It is that simple that pure, easy or hard to do and be. If you hadn't already heard, if you hadn't already noticed, my daughter was pregnant and continued to work for me almost to the day of delivery, not that she had to but because she wanted to. Everything had to be perfect. Every food item had to be filled with love. This is her signature statement. This is her glory, her pride and her love to work on a daily basis next to her dad, me. It is this love of me by her and my love for her that I share. It is this love that we have for each other as well as with our customers that help create the type of store that keeps our customers coming back and back. It is like an extended family that keep growing and growing.

It is this on this note that I share this month's feature story: the birth of Siyanna Jade, my daughter Maya's first child. It was one of those crazy Thursdays where I was one person shy and barely able to keep up with the amount of customers coming into the store. It was a type of day where the first thing in the morning I put on my special shirt. I knew deep down to the very core of my being that after nine months and three days my daughter was going to give birth sometime today. I also knew it was going to be later than sooner since my daughter knew I was literally working one person short and she really didn't want me to leave early. We have this connection of love and respect for the other. We have this connection of 100% acceptance of the other with all the flaws, with all the idiosyncrasies and with all the imperfections. We are both connected by the most important ingredient; the love of the other, no matter what.

These were my circumstances for knowing. These were her circumstances for doing the right thing for herself and her body. My daughter was diagnosed with a strep infection, which by law requires a penicillin IV solution before the birth. It was one of those things that made my blood cringle and my words lived with animosity for the medical system that desperately needs to be overhauled and reviewed from a perspective of what is best for the patient. My daughter also dreaded the penicillin so much so that she drove herself to excellence in everything she ate and more importantly everything she thought. This, my friends, is the secret for exuberant health; not so much what we eat but more importantly how we treat the food that we eat. Maya did just that. Every moment was an action of love. Her magical being created love for whoever came into her presence. It is on this special circumstance that she waited and waited for her delivery to be of love and only love and without chemical interference. Maya began her labor approximately 3:00 pm on a Thursday afternoon April 27th. Maya knew of her body's innate wisdom. Maya knew of the dangers of penicillin. Maya instinctively knew what to do. She did what any mother would do. She began her deep breathing. She trusted the laws of nature to guide her. My friends there is no handbook on exactly what it is a woman experiences the first time she gives birth. There is just a 'knowing". What holds true for pregnancy also holds true for sickness. There is a tendency not to trust, not to call on the innermost wisdom of one's knowledge as a guide to determine what is best for us.

Thus began Maya 's story of her labor and the birth of her daughter. There were so many things she knew and so many things she didn't know. Maya knew she didn't want to go to the hospital to early. Maya knew she didn't want the penicillin in her body or anywhere near her newborn child. Maya also knew that she was not only scared but also afraid of the unknown. Maya's labor pain began around at 3:00. My friends, this is where the real learning begins. This is where the real test of the unknown begins. My friends, this is the part where one has to trust their innermost wisdom. Maya began the deep breathing. She began having longer contractions. She trusted her own wisdom.   The labor progressed for two hours. It was at this point the childbirth instructor gave the final whistle. As quoted, "off to the hospital we go". At 5:30 pm after two and a half hours of being in labor, nine months of pregnancy, Maya was ready to give birth to her first child. This, my friends, is the miracle of life. This, my friends, is how we fight disease. This, my friends, is how we beat the odds of ever getting a disease. Follow your heart, trust your instinct and allow nature to take its course.

Maya arrived at the hospital at 6:10 pm about 10 minutes after I closed the store. She felt safe and secure in her position as a woman and a mother to be. As soon as Maya stepped out of the car, she had the urgency to push as if sirens of warning were on a one-day strike. Maya desperately wanted to push. She instinctively knew that the baby was coming and it was coming out at breakneck speed (whatever that means). Maya instinctively knew that she needed to get to the delivery room fast. Linda, the childbirth instructor, who was at her side grabbed and I do mean grabbed a hospital wheelchair. She placed Maya in it and began running. A call to the delivery room was put on stand bye. Joe, Maya's boyfriend, who was just parking the car and strolling into the hospital, was immediately rushed into the delivery room to watch Maya give birth to her first child at 6:18 pm.

This, my friends, is the miracle of miracles. This, my friends, is the miracle of love, the miracle of healing, and the miracle of what it takes to not only heal ourselves but to heal the country. I stand in total salute for my daughter's love, which she so elegantly shares so freely to those around. I stand in total salute to honor my daughter as being totally blessed on a moment-to-moment basis as she so lovingly reminds me what it takes to be of health and purity on that level. I give thanks for her being.

Love, Dad

"Moving forward without thinking creates freedom without anxiety's afterthoughts."

5 Fruit Smoothie:

Just add H2O

Colon Cancer
written October 1, 2001

Marches to victory flanked by terror
An army moves forward while drugs destroy the other side
It was victory in autumn, death by March
A woman is honor without living tomorrow
We cry, we weep, a nation does not understand
Battling colon cancer starts from fighting within

This week's newsletter starts amid the battle, watching the rubble being hauled away. It was a week that wrenched the whole county. It started with no one really caring what flags were, what flags meant. It ended with over 5,000 lives lost in 4 terrorist air attacks that were not meant to kill the enemy but destroy its people. So it is on this note that I begin writing about colon cancer. This is about tears I shed, the stories I heard, the survivors I saw, and the victims I didn't see. It's about a city in turmoil. It's about every day bringing another heartache, another scare, another one of the surreal atmospheres that life is being played on the mountain layers of ice. From whenst I begin to whereist I go, colon caner strikes hard also. There are 56,000 lives lost yearly. The reason I am writing this letter on this topic is because I read about just one woman dying this year. There was a big article titled, "Women's group president loses battle with cancer."

The woman, we'll call her Anita, could have died anywhere from anything, and nothing could have been said; or she could have died at the young age of 51 in the twin towers in NYC and everyone would have lauded her a hero, a victim, too young to die. We see her picture, we see her smile, we see her determination, and we see her love of life. The headlines haunt me. "Loses battle with cancer." The article states, "For five years she was battling colon cancer." I ask why? I ask where were her guardian angels? Where were her maternal instincts? The battle she fought wasn't a battle. It was a slow death using was weapons that were contraindicated for her well-being. "When she was on cancer fighting drugs." In my mind, all drugs are poison. Dr. George H. Malkamus states in God's Way to Ultimate Health, "Health cannot be restored by taking drugs. Drugs cannot rebuild the cells of the body. The body is self-healing." So I continue writing with a heavy heart, and my tears are being shed for those who died in NYC. My hands are tied for that victory is beyond my control. The only thing I can give is support for those that died, those who are going to die, and those who lost loved ones, and pray for the wisdom of God to share his eternal bliss to all those who walk the earth.

My silence stands in salute of those that died. My fury is raised to battle for those that died of colon cancer. In that battle I have a right to chose the weapon wisely, to elaborate, to share, to convey heart-felt emotion to those survivors of Anita who were not given the proper information so cancer would not only not have conquered, it never would have happened.

So I begin my research starting with, "What is cancer?" In The Cancer Answer, Albert Carter writes, " Cancer is not a disease. It is a naturally occurring condition." As explained further, "In every instance, cancer cells are caused by mutation of the genes in the DNA that control both cell growth and cell reproduction." At first reading, that sounds pretty scary, meaning, like you and me can develop this fairly easily. But the truth, if a truth does exist, as quoted from the Cancer Answer is that, "In a healthy body it's (cancer) close to impossible." I hear these words and I see the headlines. I read the statistics according to the National Vital Statistics Reports Volume 47 no9 of 1996. There were 539,533 deaths due to cancer. In 2000 there were 56,000 deaths due to colon cancer. On August 29 at the age of 51, Anita died of colon cancer, which, according to Albert Carter, is almost impossible to get.

So we begin to look at the cancer fighting drugs. The American medical community's choice for fighting this natural occurrence is not natural. The death rate upon hearing those words is 95% for all victims of live cancer died within six months.

That's the good news, for the word drugs in a medical sense means healing. As of 1998, there were approximately 40 cancer drugs of which 26 were commercially available. Let's make no mistake. Anita had colon cancer for 5 years. She was given only one option - Drug Therapy. If she were given another more radical approach she may have seen some different results. Dr. Neal Barnard, author of Food for Life, stated, "People who include fruits and vegetables in their daily dietary habit lower many forms of cancer including lung, breast, and colon." Is there an awakening here? I ask especially because I read at the beginning of the paragraph where he states, "Oxygen molecules that become unstable are called free radicals." The question next questions then become, what is a free radical, what causes it, and how can we prevent it? So like a handshake that can't stop its momentum, the search for the cure can lead to many levels of understanding.

By definition, free radicals are unstable, destructive molecules that are found in vegetable oil, fish oil, and iron. All stimulate the production of free radicals. Once again, according to Dr. Neal Barnard, "Vegetables and fruits also provide antioxidants to help neutralize the free radicals that are produced." Dr. Barnard, as president of the Physician Committee for Responsible Medicine along with other world renown scientists Dr. Denis Burkitt (medical pioneer who discovered the value of fiber) and Dr. T. Colin Campbell (Cornell University biochemist who headed the prestigious China Health Study) all talk passionately that DIET not drugs is key for dramatic improvement in health.

So the conflicts begin. Who is right? Who is wrong? In 1955 the search for cancer drugs began its journey. There have been almost 1,500,000 chemical compounds tested. Of these chemical compounds, there are currently 40 cancer drugs around of which 26 are commercially available as of 1998. The National Cancer Institute (NCI) criteria for accepting these drug compounds states, "Any chemical that interferes with the mechanism of natural cell division is a candidate. Most cancer drugs interact with the genetic material in a cell, so anything that keeps cells from dividing naturally might be classed as a cancer drug."

So we review the words of Anita's battle. "Even when she was sick and even when she was on cancer fighting drugs…" And we close our eyes and repeat the NCI's criteria for accepting chemical compounds. I sit in my chair in disbelief for Anita was given the wrong option. She knew the battle but not the enemy from without. Her battle weapons were her poisons for worse not better.

Below is a list of chemical compounds that are used to fight cancer approved by National Cancer Institute as of 1998 (taken from Cancer Answer): Mustard Gas: A highly toxic gas used in UU2. Its vapor is extremely poisonous. Some side effects cause cancer of the bronchi, lungs, larynx, and trachea Nitrogen Mustard: Used for treating malignancies has shown to cause cancer years after being used to combat cancer 5 Flourouricil: This chemical interferes with an enzyme that the body requires to build DNA Methotrexate: An antivitamin that has similar qualities to folic acid. Eventually, the cell chooses methotrexate instead of folic acid causing the cell to die Procarbazine: This drug nicks the DNA and breaks it. When the DNA chain is destroyed a cell cannot reproduce Bacterial Compounds: These substances slip between the strands of DNA and prevent its copying function from working.

I could go on, but I won't. These cancer-fighting chemicals, besides being expensive, take a tremendous toll on the body. As stated in the Cancer Answer, "The chemicals attack all quickly dividing cells, healthy as well as malignant." The side effects of these chemicals are devastating including diarrhea, vomiting, anemia, and hair loss, which explains why Anita was sick and suffering for 5 years, fighting chemical treatments and surgery.

You would think that all this suffering was necessary, even to extend her life one extra day or one extra month or one extra year. According to the New England Journal of Medicine of 1984, "Colon cancer victims don't live any longer when they receive chemotherapy along with the standard surgical removal of their tumors."

It's my usual late-night writing time (past 11pm), and I debate to myself whether or not I should forward this letter to the memorial fund set up for Anita that is asking for money for colon cancer research headed by NCI. Would they get mad at me? Should I have used Anita's real name? I ponder.

Dr. Samuel Epstein, The Politics of Cancer, feels, "The entire decision making process of the NCI is slanted in favor of chemotherapy and basic research." What does all this information mean? What do these conflicts in cancer treatment indicate? Is there a conspiracy that allows for 540,000 cancer deaths a year?

We think about Anita's death. We think about the chemical compounds that are given in the name of healing. We think about why those in charge of cancer prevention choose drugs over fruit and vegetable therapy. Thousands, millions, and billions of dollars are being generated by this system that is being kept in place for the sake of the pharmaceutical industry.

So Anita dies in a battle, and no on says a word about the identity of the real killer. No one is even aware that these truths exist.

The truth is being squashed because there is no money to be exchanged. In the December 1983 issue there was an article that stated, "Too few people all on intimate and friendly terms with each other are in change of handing out the large sum of money to each other."

I write, I think while time passes. It's past 12:30am, and there is ever so much more to say. As we delve into colon cancer, the causes, the side effects, and the reasons why as years pass statistically it not only doesn't get any better, colon cancer gets worse. The facts are not being shared. The causes are not being shared. The treatments are not being shared. I sit in silence thinking what words are s allow? What words are powerful? What words do I have to use in order for people to get it? With each moment passing, with each moment that this information is not being shared, another story can be written. A story with a face dying of a failed battle plan, a brave soul who fought a brave way. And as long as there is the same battle plan with the same weapons there will be the same story: victims of life who lose their battle with cancer.

I think not of losing but of winning. I think of George Malkamus who developed colon cancer 23 years ago. I think that if he had not heard of the raw food possibilities he too would have chosen the same path as Anita.

So rather than losing his life to cancer he went on to win and reach the good life. He chose fruits and vegetables over drugs. His DNA did not get destroyed. He did not develop the side effects, the vomiting, the weight loss, the low energy, the hair loss, the loss of cells, or the loss of life. In 1976, at the age of 42, George was told he had colon cancer. A tumor was found the size of a baseball underneath his left ribcage. He chose his weapons of war. Make no mistake. George was diagnosed with cancer, in which mutant cells develop by our body's mechanism that have no practical use by our body other than to destroy other healthy cells. So George went to war by changing his diet. As he stated in God's Way to Ultimate Health, he changed his diet to, "Raw fruits and vegetables and lots of fresh carrot juice." As time passed, so did his colon cancer.

Although I'm excited about continuing this same pattern of thought, although I just finished eating a pound of grapes and having tons of usable energy remaining, the clock is approaching 1am. I have to be up early, 6:30am, for a Saturday morning class on raw food and healing. I too weigh my options. Put the pen down, turn off the light, and hopefully finish this tomorrow. Right now sleep awaits me.

It's not the next day, but two days later, for those who keep track. And believe it or not, there are those who keep track because they ask me what was so important on Saturday that I couldn't continue. To all those who are going to ask me that, I'm sorry. I got busy. Tonight is Sunday around 11:30pm. I continue. It's kind of hard, but it's not an option. There are truths about life that have to be written. There are truths about colon cancer that have to be shared. There are drugs given that are supposed to help the fight against cancer. But if a truth exists, it stands to reason that it should be obvious to everyone. But it's not. There are 540,000 cancer deaths and 56,000 colon cancer deaths. There are 26 compound chemicals whose side effects devastate one's internal organs. There are fruits and vegetables, which have shown to be effective in not only slowing down cancer but also preventing it. So we read these facts, we throw them against the wall, and we pray, for each of us has our own path and our own choice. There is nothing that I can say or write once somebody makes up his or her mind to choose the medical option. I, Arnold, having done my due diligence in researching most of the major diseases, including colon cancer, will use every means at my disposal to share this information to prevent another person from suffering for 5 years of trying to win a battle that can't be won when using the wrong weapons.

I thank you for your time,
Arnold

References:
Food for Life by Dr. Neal Barnard, M.D.
The Cancer Answer by Albert Carter
Alternative Medicine
God's Way to Ultimate Health by Dr. George Malkamus
"Women's Group President Loses Battle with Cancer," newspaper article by Merry Eisenstadt

"Me, myself, and I, never ever alone."

Creating the recipe is the responsibility of the reader:

Give me 5 recipes using 5 fruits.

Commitment to Health
written May 8, 2005

When speaking of health without sickness the answer is easy, everything that is supposed to happen happens. Everything that is supposed to be actually is. It is the game of life. To be healthy requires commitment. To be happy and content also requires that commitment to excellence. It was my 47th day or thereabout when I lost my vision in the left eye after a freak accident. I could have chosen a cataract removal, which by all medical standards would have alleviated the situation. What I could have and what I did was based on doing what is best for me. I chose self-healing. I chose going to the utmost extreme of healing myself against all odds. I was paying the ultimate sacrifice. In my particular case, it was worth it. I am now conscious of almost everything I do to create healing, beginning from what I eat in the morning to what time I go to bed. All these little things that at one time were non-entities in a daily ritual now rise to great significance. When we speak of excellence in not only the things we say and do but also the little innuendos that represent our daily being.

The basis of our soul is based on that understanding of doing the right thing. It is on that basis that the health and excellence is based. It is on that basis that we as humans have to be of love, speak of love and give that love not only to others but more important to ourselves. It is on that level of honesty and truth that our body understands not only the mind but also the heart, the ideal of simplicity and keeping it real. It is on that level that the body demands the fruit and veggies given to us by the universe. It is on that level of simplicity that the body responds. It is on that level that what we consume on a daily basis ultimately determines our health and our wealth not only for ourselves but also for all future generations. I gathered this knowledge and became conscious of what I not only put in my body but what I do with it. In other words, another form of self-healing and self-responsibility is exercise, exercise and more exercise. These are some of the steps necessary for a return to health.

So I take this wisdom and sleep on it. The body requires a tremendous amount of sleep. As the sun rises so too does the sun set. Our body functions with that rhythm. I now go bed early and rise early. It is a period of 12 hours daily where food is not eaten. It is a period of time where rest becomes the cornerstone of healing. As my life searches for that excellence in a journey that will see many up's and down's of what works best. It is at that point where emotions of the past come roaring in, words like sabotage and compromise become everyday passwords that create blockages of what is really necessary for total rejuvenation. I write and I live with my daily decisions.

"We have no idea how lucky we are. Every 75-trillion cells in our body are working ferociously, keeping us alive and happy without ever a mistake."

Rockin, no thinkin'

Just pick any 5

Done deal

Constipation

written June 7, 2001

It was the sunset of our dreams. It became the magnet that allows the stars to rise and the moon to fall. It became the envy of every girl. It was the first wish of every boy. It was a hush hush secret - not to be shared by anyone. For the truth, if it was spoken would shed a different light about a naughty word that's never meant to be spoken. So we begin this week newsletter on constipation. To those that I promised, to those whom I just heard of their tales, to those who would never dream of sharing, to those, here it goes.

It's a bright sunny afternoon in May and I just finished reading "The Hygiene Care of Constipation" for the third time. There were some definitely brow-raising statements which put a new slant to the word constipation and how it is perceived and how it is treated. By those who know, by those who think they know to those who don't know. Also to those who don't know, nor think. Judging from what I read, if it can be taken as a truth. The colon's main function is acting as a reservoir until such time the body decides to expel the contents. Digestion takes place in the mouth and small intestine. The body in, its infinite wisdom, uses the nutrition it derives from the food and passes the rest along through a peristaltic or wave-like movement, until it reaches the first yard of the large intestine. Just as the beat of the heart or blink of the eye, our body will continue moving what it doesn't need along until it is expelled.

The colon is not packed with debris- that requires irrigation-enemas to remove it. In fact, according to Dr. Shelton, who ran a Health School and clinic for over forty years states those "people who have taken enemas and colonic irrigation over a long period of time are in worse condition than any other class of colons I have see." If we take a step back and examine the colon- not like Shelton- but like a layman who researches information on his own, like me, we'd discover that the large intestine is 6ft long and 2 inches wide, shaped like an inverted horseshoe. Its primary function is to absorb water, from the small intestine then expel the remainder from the body.

Where does constipation come in to play? In the small intestine which is approximately twenty -two feet long and 1.5 inches wide. A grand total of 28ft of intestinal track believe it or not contains trillions of bacteria. According to World Medicine including " E Coli, candida albicans or yeast and lacto bacteria." To add more human bewilderment to this already complex system, every two to four days the entire lining of the mucus membrane are replaced by a new set of cells. Where do they go and where do they come from? Is constipation really a threat or a cure?

According to Dr. Walker he refers to constipation as "the number one affliction underlying nearly every ailment." Dr. Walker, who wrote "Colon Health ;the Key to Vibrant Life", espouses the same words as Dr. Shelton. They both agree that " Mucus is created to encapsulate the waste of certain foods such as meat, dairy, white flour and other processed foods." He further explains that this process of constipation is a defense mechanism so that the waste material which is toxic does not flow into the blood stream. Thank your body when this occurs. The short term effect of this toxic waste getting into the blood stream include pimples, sore throats, colds, hay fevers, sinus, eye and ear problems. Long term effects according to Dr. Walker are degeneration or cancer in vital organs.

What are the options? What are the cures? Who do we listen to? As the sun rises so as it sets. As a baby is born so will that baby die. In life as in death there is a rhythm of wisdom that stands still for no one. An answer of time and element that brings joy to breath and relief of just letting go. At this moment I refuse to refer to the Merck Manual for answers. They have a language that speaks of drugs, greed and diplomas in learning to repeat the answers that are given. I refused to research other medical options for the answers are the same cause they evolve from the same thought process. That is our body intellect composed of trillions of cells, having zillions of functions and operating under the power of a supreme energy does not know from what it does to what it is to do. That the medical profession hidden by the years of school, books and degrees can only solve the health of our soul. That can only happen by a pill of synthetic origin or a shot of more disputable origin for these were the only answers given to them in their 8-10 years of Drug education. So these thought processes are banished from this. On that note we continue reciting more raw food options and possibilities:

According to Dr. Shelton "Constipation is a symptom of the patient's overall toxemia. The only remedy suggested by him is to remove the cause. (Refer back to Dr. Walker's statements and replace it with the 10 Energy Enhancers)

1. Pure air- fresh country air from 20 minutes to one hour per day
2. Pure water- distilled is best but filter will do
3. Adequate rest and sleep
If you are tired, take it as a gift to rest more
4. Ideal Diet- a mostly fruit and vegetable, nut and seed diet
5. Right Temperature
6. Natural Sunlight
7. Regular Exercise- 20 minutes to 45 min. daily, 3-5 times a week
8. Emotional Balance
9. Nurturing Relationship
10. For the constipation suffering- emphasis on fasting

Dr. Walker recommends regular use of colonic irrigation, a statement that was vigorously opposed by Dr. Shelton. "In God's Way" by Dr. George H. Malkamus a vegetarian diet of at least 75 to 85 percent raw fruit and vegetable is strongly recommended before using any Herbal concoctions. We at Arnold's Way take the same position unless absolutely necessary you feel a strong desire to take an enema-irrigation herbal concoction.

According to Kate Hauck a Certified Classical Homeopath, constipated people are different from one another. And whether a person is over-controlled, over-anxious, too diligent at everything, chronically frightened, chronically unsure, ashamed, embarrassed, disgusted, or intolerant of strange bathrooms, I will base my homeopathic prescription on the bodymind whole. Then, between eating better and taking the right homeopathic remedy for them, their bowels go from disease to ease. The whole person does, too.

In self testing your colon according to Teresa and Toni Schumacherlund who wrote "Cleansing the Body and Colon for a Happier and Healthier You" states "once we have eaten a meal we should be able to eliminate the waste from that food within 16-24 hours." She notes, "the average elimination time in America is 96 hours." To test your transit time eat some beets or drink fresh beet juice and then wait. We at Arnold's Way as always agree with Dr. Shelton's Hygiene View of eating. "Remove the cause and the body will heal itself."

Thank you for you time,
Arnold

References

- "God's Way to Ultimate Health" by Dr. George Malkmus
- "The Life Food Recipe Book" by Annie Jubb and David Jubb PH.D
- "Common Health Sense" by Dr. Herbert M. Shelton and edited by Victoria Bidwell
- "World Medicine" by Tom Monte and Editors of East West Natural Health

"The great understanding of life is realizing that every moment alive is Vacation City, no matter where or when."

How's this happening?

Picking just 5 fruits & creating 25 meals, duh

Crutches
written March 1, 2001

This week has been an exciting week at Arnold's Way Raw Cafe . . . which is nothing new since its always exciting & always fun! The reason is very simple: Arnold, a raw foodist, is happily creating new challenges while at the same time, following through with old commitments.

Happiness.

To be happy -- joyful -- does not have to be an evolving hope, but rather is a God-given & Natural birthright. We as a people, a town, a country, are facing a danger from within -- a force that can no longer be fought with guns or tanks. It is a force which battles our own sense of happiness, by invading our health, well-being, and inner peace. It is a force to be reckoned with, as we face daily challenges in our lives and make choices accordingly. What is this force?

It is a disheartening of the spirit.

How does it make its mark in our daily lives?

It is common practice for people to rely on what we call "crutches." There are everyday crutches of cigarette-smoking, coffee-drinking, drugs, and stimulants that people feel the need to consume just in order to finish their days . . . just to maintain a level of energy sufficient enough to "hang in there."

As a health food store owner, I hear the echoes of brain drain everyday: complaints about a lack of energy, feeling down, or even a barely uplifting "hanging in there." Is there truly a difference between feeling great without drugs or stimulants, or simply "hanging in there" with low energy? What makes the difference? Do people recognize the need to nourish their own vitality through healthy means vs. the means so readily available over-the-counter or at the coffee shop?

Our brains have an understanding so clear and coherent that there are absolutely no mistakes in its daily operation. There is not one mistake from our moment of birth to our time of death. Imagine for just a minute if we -- the you's and the me's -- were transformed to being just brains. We as human beings are composed of about 75,000,000,000 cells, all directed by the one, the only -- brain. Just one cell in our bodies have enough intelligence to fill 40,000 books with factual information from which our brains operate. So imagine that we are transformed to being only the higher center of bodily control we call the brain. Imagine the concentrated ability the consciousness that our brains possess. Our brains are able to consciously remove bodily substance and change it into cranial matter. Our brains have the ability to direct and move toxic substances in an effort to preserve one's vitality -- one's life force. Our brains are our gift of Life. They are the decision-makers, the coordinators of important vital bodily function. Our brains lay the foundation for daily decisions and choices by which we function and manage to maintain, sustain, and attain HAPPINESS.

Thus, when we experience brain drain, or a loss of vital energy, we must force ourselves to take a deep look at what choices we make on a daily level which are contributing to this lack of energy.

The challenges of our busy lives, coupled with the use of "crutches" in order to live up to those challenges, create a situation in which are ironically diffusing our vital energy in an attempt to nourish it. What do I mean? We bombard our bodies and brains with hot coffee, alcohol, cigarettes, processed foods, and other strong stimulants and drugs. These methods are considered to be heavy weights upon our body's well-being. Imagine the brain-the ultimate general -- and its constant barrage of these toxic substances. It has no choice but to feel depressed & rejected, and to adjust its levels of energy accordingly. We as a people are faced with the choices of these substances everyday. And in choosing to consume these substances, we are consistently dragging our levels of energy lower and lower until we are just "hanging in there." Arnold of Arnold's Way understands these concepts. And you know what he says?

Well, I don't want to "just hang in there." I want to feel great. I want to be happy. I want to feel energized by Life on a daily level.

A body needs the proper conditions for health in order to fulfill its birth right of joy and happiness. We at Arnold's Way do not want to PREACH the benefits of changing one's diet to mostly raw, but we feel the need to SHARE information in an effort to enable each of us to make the right decisions regarding our own sense of happiness and well-being.

So thanks for reading and listening and please stop in for some more sharing and caring ... Arnold's Way, of course!

"Magic balloon, yellow daffodils, a blind monkey all join forces – happy together in the land of make-believe."

5 Yellow Fruit:

So easy to pick

"Love conquers all.
God is good.
No questions asked.
Everything is
understood."

Take your chances
and choose without
fear:

Any 5 fruits

"We laugh. We cry. We think. We wonder what's important and what's not. How cliche is this? It's life, duh."

What Do You Want?

Fruit all the way.

5 Fruit =
5 Dollars &
5 Minutes to make

"My forever mantra – lean, mean, fighting machine. The words are the glue that keep me going day in & day out."

Done deal, doing it.

Choosing 5 fruit.

"In reality, the end is always just the beginning."

Almost done but not good enough -

5 fruits can equal 25 meals. MMM.

"Don't judge
the stop sign
that speaks
the truth."

My time is up.

5 fruits
5 meals
Or, exponentially
so much more

"Goal oriented with success requires a plan of action & a date of completion."

Worst recipe book ever, or maybe the best.

"The great misunderstanding of life is by not knowing. Eating dead animals affects every part of our soul and spirit with lifelong detrimental effects, and the saddest part is that 95% of people don't care."

This is 3 books in 1. Which one is the key?

"What you don't know is more powerful than what you don't know."

Don't stop till it's over, or in reality, it's never over.

5 fruits can equal so many meals.

"The greatest life journey begins with your first step towards the alignment of your truth."

Crazy stuff in choosing which 5 fruits & which 25 meals. Is it possible?

"True love always starts with I. Let's not forget when thinking of starting a new romance."

Deciding which is the hardest part,

Any 5.

"Thinking too hard of the most correct almost always leads to stagnant constipated thought process. Just do it with no worries or concern of the outcome."

Choose wisely. The reader creates his own way.

"There is no right or wrong, just a discussion on differences."

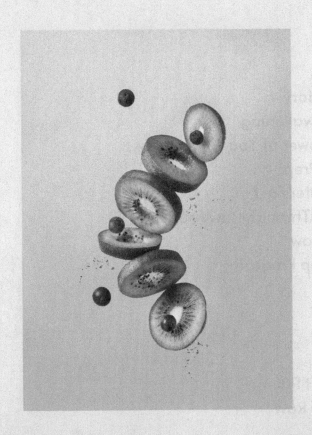

Fruit is God's food we are designed to eat.

Arnold's Other Works

LITERATURE

-Low Fat Raw Vegan Lifestyle Regeneration
-Johnny NuCell
-Why Johnny NuCell Feels So Good
-The Way of Arnold
-The Many Ways of Arnold
-Seven-Point-Seven
-Arnold's Way Essays on Health
-14 Days at Tanglewood
-Arnold's Way Healing Success Stories
-Arnold's Way Recipe Book
-Arnold's Way Childproof Recipes for Everyone
-Banana Power to the Rescue
-Johnny NuCell's Big Plan
-W.T.H. Poetry Book
-76 My Best Year Until Next
-This Recipe Book Sucks
-On Purpose

FILM

-Tommy's Story
-Breast Cancer Awakening
-Raw Power: The Power of You
-Raw Food Prep
-My 21-Day Water Fast
-Healthy Living and Healing Through Raw Foods
-30 Days Raw
-Arnold's Seven Step Program

ALBUMS

-Can't Sing, Can't Rhyme
-The Power of Raw

Arnold's Other Works

More Albums Coming Soon to Spotify...

-God's Rules for Living the Dream
-Doing It - Banana Power to the Rescue
-Rockin to My Bodies Tunes
-Desperation - Transformation to Exhilaration

CONNECT WITH ARNOLD:

Arnoldsway.com

Instagram: @arnoldsway

Facebook: Arnold's Way Vegetarian Raw Cafe and Health Center
&
Arnold N. Kauffman

YouTube: Arnold's Way Channel (Over 3,000 videos!)

Made in the USA
Columbia, SC
07 July 2024

38135192R00043